The REAL Scientist Investigates...
ELECTRICITY

Peter Riley

SEA-TO-SEA

Mankato Collingwood London

Contents

Striking Electricity

Do you ever wonder why you sometimes get zapped with a shock when you touch metal objects on a dry day? The small sparks are caused by the release of electricity. The largest and most dangerous spark of all is lightning. It flashes from clouds to the ground, and has the power to kill.

Real scientists discovered tiny particles called atoms, which make up everything around us. These are made of even tinier particles—electrons and protons. Electrons carry a negative electric charge and protons carry a positive electric charge. Sparks, such as lightning, are caused by the movement of electrons through the air.

Sometimes, when you touch something metal, the shock you feel is the release of electrical energy. A tiny spark is generated, just like this one.

WARNING!
Never use household electricity (from an outlet or socket) for experiments. It is much more powerful than any electricity stored in a battery and can kill—just like lightning!

▲ The electricity we use every day is more stable than lightning. You'll never see a spark of electricity, because it "flows" safely along wires—but it's there!

How to Be a Real Scientist

Real scientists look at our world and try to understand it by thinking about it and performing experiments. You can be a real scientist, too! Just look at each topic, read the "Get Going" section, and then start experimenting.

Set Up a Science Box

Find a large box, then look through the pages in this book to find out all the things you will need in order to get going on each activity. Gather them up and put them in your science box.

Use These Science Skills

▶ **Observe**
Look carefully at whatever you are investigating.

▶ **Predict**
Guess what will happen before you experiment.

▶ **A fair test**
If you are comparing something in your experiment, make sure you keep everything the same in your tests except for one thing—the thing you are investigating.

▶ **Science notebook**
You will need a science notebook in which to put information about your investigations.

▶ **Record**
Write down what happened and perhaps make a drawing in your science notebook. You could take photographs, too, or make a video using a camcorder or cellphone.

▶ **Make a conclusion**
Compare what happened with your prediction and see if you were right. It does not matter if you were wrong because it helps you rethink your ideas.

▶ **Experiments and answers**
Follow the steps in the experiments carefully. Use your science skills. There may be extra experiments and a question for you to try. Check all your observations, ideas, and answers on pages 28–29.

▶ **What went wrong?**
Science experiments are famous for going wrong—sometimes. If your experiment does not seem to work, check the "What's wrong?" section to help you make it right.

Supercharged

Some types of electricity can be a real pain, such as when a piece of plastic "sticks" to your finger and you can't shake it off. Blame the protons and electrons. Atoms normally have the same number of positive protons and negative electrons. But rubbing some materials can change this balance and create an electric charge.

▼ The protons clump together at the center of the atom, called the nucleus. The electrons move around the nucleus like the planets move around the Sun, but they move much faster—almost at the speed of light.

Normally, positive and negative charges cancel each other out—this is called neutral. But when some materials are rubbed, they lose or gain electrons. A material that loses electrons becomes positively charged with electricity. A material that gains electrons becomes negatively charged with electricity.

Get Going

What happens when a material is rubbed and becomes charged with electricity? What does it do to things around it? Try this experiment to find out.

Electrical Fleas

Science Box

The clear plastic lid from a CD case, four pieces of modeling clay about ¼ in. (1 cm) high, some yarn, a sheet of paper, material for "fleas" (a small strip of styrofoam cut from a styrofoam cup, glitter, a small piece of tissue paper, six pieces of puffed rice cereal).

1 Tear the tissue paper and styrofoam into about ten very small pieces and put them on the paper. Sprinkle on some glitter.

2 Break up the pieces of puffed rice cereal, but avoid making them into powder. Add them to the paper.

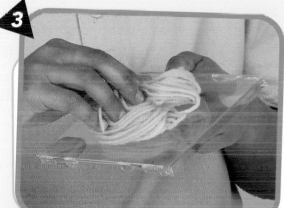

3 Attach each piece of modeling clay to a corner of the CD lid and rub the lid quickly with the yarn for a minute.

4 Place the lid over the paper and watch the "fleas." Then rub the top of the lid again, remove the yarn, and watch what happens.

▶ **Observe**
What happens to the "fleas" when you place the lid over them? What happens to the "fleas" when you rub the lid again and then remove the yarn?

▶ **Predict**
What might happen if you raise the CD lid up higher and start again?

▶ **Record**
Take a photograph of all your "fleas" stuck to your lid.

▶ **What's wrong?**
Nothing happening? Rub the CD lid for longer.

▶ **Think about it**
The electricity generated by rubbing stays in one place on the object. It is called static electricity. How could you tell if something might be charged with static electricity? Now see pages 8–9.

Fantastic Static

The surface of a charged material is covered in extra electrons or protons. They don't move, so real scientists say the material is charged with static electricity, but when an object of the opposite charge is brought near, the two objects attract—**zappp!**

Static electricity can be used in some processes, such as spray painting a car. The spray of liquid paint is positively charged and the car is negatively charged, so that almost all the paint is attracted to the car and sticks to the charged surface.

▲ This is an electrofilter (everything except the red-checked chimneys). Electrofilters have been fitted to many chimneys for years. They use static electricity to remove most of the tiny smoke particles from the air.

▼ Static electricity helps give this car an even coat of paint.

Getting Going

When some materials are rubbed, they become charged with static electricity and they can make things move. You can make a simple electrical instrument, called a versorium, to see if different materials become charged when they are rubbed.

A Charge Detector

1

Stick the modeling clay in the center of the plastic dish.

2

Place the pencil in the modeling clay with the point sticking up.

![Science Box]

Science Box

A plastic dish, modeling clay, a pencil, a piece of aluminum foil 5 in. long by 1½ in. wide (12 x 4 cm), some yarn, a roll of adhesive tape, a selection of materials such as a balloon, a wooden spoon, a mug, a plastic ruler, a stone, a ceramic bowl, a glass marble.

3

Fold the strip of aluminum foil down the middle, place it over the point of the pencil, and bend it slightly so that it balances and can turn easily.

4

Rub each material one at a time with yarn and bring it close to one end of the foil strip. If the material is charged, the strip will move.

▶ Fair test
Rub each material the same number of times before testing it with the versorium.

▶ Observe
Did each material make the foil move the same amount?

▶ Record
Make a movie of your versorium in action as you test different materials.

▶ What's wrong?
Foil didn't move for any of them? You may have pressed it down on the pencil too hard. Reset it on the pencil and make sure that it can turn freely.

▶ Extra experiment
Put a roll of adhesive tape next to the versorium. Move it away and pull some tape off the roll and, without cutting it, bring it close to the foil. What do you see and conclude?

▶ Think about it
If two balloons were hung on string, and a person rubbed their hair on both of them, what would happen when the balloons were brought close together?

Conducting Current

All materials are made from atoms, which contain electrons. In some materials, electrons can leave the atoms and move. Whenever we turn on the TV or a light, we complete a circuit and start electric current flowing. We can tell it's flowing because the screen or light goes on.

An electric current is made up of electrons and can only flow through materials that have electrons that are free to move. These materials are called conductors. Materials that have fixed electrons are called insulators, and do not allow electric currents to flow.

Get Going

In this experiment, we will make electricity flow along metal foil from a battery and then test materials in a circuit to see if they are conductors or insulators.

1 Stick the battery at one end of the cardboard with tape.

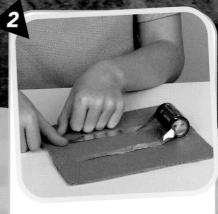

2 Stick one long piece of foil to the base of the battery and one to the cap. Twist them a little then stick them to the cardboard.

A Simple Circuit

This train is powered by electricity carried along metal overhead cables. The electricity is insulated from the ground and the train by ceramic disks.

Science Box

A piece of cardboard about 9 x 8 in. (22 x 20 cm), a piece of cardboard 3 x 1 in. (8 x 3 cm), a 1.5 V battery, two strips of aluminum foil ½ x 6 in. (1 x 16 cm), a piece of aluminum foil about ½ x 4 in. (1 x 10 cm), adhesive tape, a 3.5 V flashlight bulb (see page 14), a pencil, paper clip, ruler, a pebble.

▶ Observe

What do you see when you set up the circuit and complete it in step 3?

▶ What's wrong?

Bulb does not light or it flickers? Check all connections and make sure the bulb is pressed onto the foil strip. Check that the foil strips are not torn or split.

▶ Extra experiment

Leave a small gap between the end of the short foil strip on the bridge and the long strip of foil on the cardboard. Put items such as a metal paper clip, a plastic ruler, or a pebble, one at a time, across the gap and see if the bulb lights up.

▶ Record

Identify which materials are conductors and which are insulators and record them in a table.

▶ Think about it

If you leave the circuit connected, what will eventually happen to the battery and bulb?

3

Turn the small piece of cardboard into a "bridge" and make a hole in the middle of it using a pencil. Wrap one end of the short foil strip around the bulb case and push it into the hole. Place the bulb so that its base touches one of the long foil strips and turn the bridge so the end of the short foil touches the other long foil.

Brilliant Batteries

All batteries, from tiny, flat ones to massive super batteries, are stores of electricity. Most batteries have a number printed on them followed by a "V," for "volts." This is a measure of the battery power—the push the battery gives to the electrons as they flow around the circuit.

► Part of the world's biggest battery—ABB's battery for Fairbanks, Alaska.

Batteries can be lined up in a circuit to increase the power. For example, three 1.5 V batteries lined up correctly give the electrons a push of 4.5 volts. Power has to be controlled though—4.5 volts of electricity would "blow" a 3.5 V bulb.

Get Going

Does it matter how batteries and motors are connected into a circuit? Here are some arrangements for you to try.

1

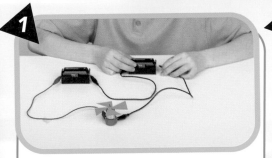

Cut two fan shapes from the cardboard. Push one fan onto a motor. Stick the motor down with clay. Make a circuit like this with the battery caps facing the same way (+ to –).

2

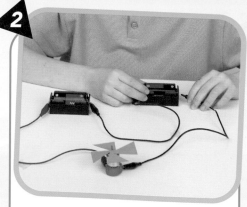

Now, make a circuit with the caps of the two batteries facing each other (– to –).

12

Positive terminal (cap)
(+)

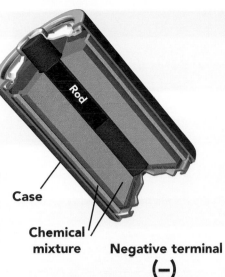

Rod

Case

Chemical mixture

Negative terminal
(–)

▶ The two important parts of a battery are the terminals. The positive terminal is at the cap and attracts negative electrons. The negative terminal is at the base and repels or pushes negative electrons.

Making Circuits

Science Box

Two batteries and holders, two motors, three connecting wires with crocodile clips, modeling clay, scissors, cardboard.

▶ **Observe**
Did the motor in step 1 spin? What happened in step 2? How did the motors spin in step 3 compared to the single motor in step 1?

▶ **Record**
Take photographs of your circuits when all the wires are connected.

▶ **What's wrong?**
Motors not moving in steps 1 and 3? Check all connections to make sure they are secure.

▶ **Extra experiment**
Repeat step 3, but this time connect one motor to the batteries and the other motor in an extra loop to the first motor (you'll need additional wires). Compare your observations to the ones you made earlier.

▶ **Predict**
What will happen if you add another battery to the circuit?

▶ **Think about it**
Why do you think batteries are available in different voltages? Why should you always align batteries correctly in an electrical appliance?

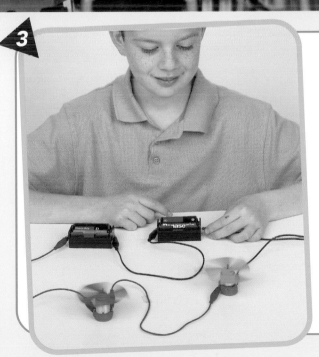

3

Make a circuit with two fans and motors in a line and two batteries with their caps facing the same way (+ to –).

Super Switches

When we turn on a TV, we use a switch. When the switch is "on," the current of electricity flows. When the switch is "off," it stops. A switch is a very simple part of a circuit and is made of two metal parts called contacts. The contacts touch only when the switch is on.

▼ Switches make our lives a lot easier. Can you imagine trying to change TV channels without them? It would be almost impossible!

▲ This is a closeup of some microswitches. They are tiny, and are hidden away in the circuits of many appliances, such as TVs.

Many switches we use every day are tiny. Microswitches are found in many electrical products, such as a computer mouse or console, because they are small and very robust. Some can be pushed over 10 million times without breaking!

Get Going

Switches make it easier to control the flow of electricity than joining wires or strips of metal foil together. Make these switches and see how they control the flow of electricity faster than before.

1

Switch 1: Stick the three pieces of cardboard together.

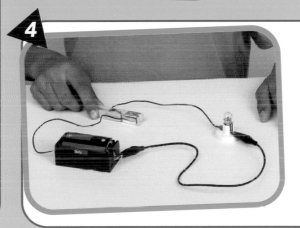
2

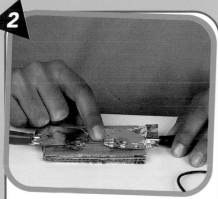

3

Switch 2: Cut two strips of foil. Stick them onto the inside of the poster board, so that when the card is shut, the foil pieces touch.

Cut two pieces of foil about 2 x 1 in. (5 x 2 cm) and pin one to the card with a thumbtack. Hook a paper clip under a thumbtack and use it to pin the second foil to the cardboard. The paper clip can swing and touch the first thumbtack.

4

Switch 3: Cover the two ends of a clothespin with foil. Strip off the coating from the two pieces of wire and stick one to each piece of foil.

▶ **Observe**
Connect switch 1 into the circuit using the photo in step 4 to help you. Swing the paper clip of switch 1, so it touches the opposite piece of foil. What happens to the bulb?

▶ **Predict**
What will happen when you replace switch 1 with switch 2 and press it together? Test your prediction. What will happen when you replace switch 2 with switch 3 and open and close the clothespin?

▶ **Record**
Take photographs of switches when they are in the circuit and letting electricity flow.

▶ **What's wrong?**
Switch not working? Check that the contacts are joined together and that all other connections in the circuit are secure.

▶ **Extra experiment**
Look at the Morse code on page 30. Use it to send a message to a friend. Give your friend the code and see if they can understand your message. Which switch works the best?

▶ **Think about it**
Could you use a piece of string to make contacts for a switch?

Security System

A security system helps protect valuable objects, such as the Crown Jewels (below). If the circuit is broken, a special switch lets electricity flow, which activates lots of antitheft devices.

▲ This is St. Edward's Crown, part of the Crown Jewels of the reigning monarch of Great Britain. They are protected in the Tower of London by electronic beams and motion sensors, which trigger alarms and close steel shutters.

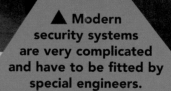

▲ Modern security systems are very complicated and have to be fitted by special engineers.

Get Going

Set up this jewel-thief challenge for your friends in this investigation. Make this simple security system so you can tell when anyone lifts the lid on the box of goodies. See if your friends can get into the box without the bulb going out—and without damaging the box.

Make a Security System

1

Cut a hole in the side of the box and push the bulb in. Connect the bulb into a circuit with a battery and two pieces of foil for a switch. Test the circuit. Now, cut a slot in each side of the lid.

Science Box

A cardboard box with a double-flap lid, a battery, a bulb, two strips of aluminum foil, goodies, three wires with crocodile clips, adhesive tape.

2

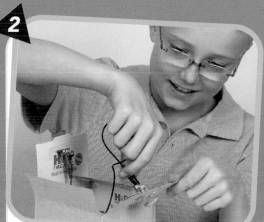

Put the circuit in the box. Push each foil strip up through one of the lid slots.

3

Close the box lid. Touch the pieces of foil together to complete the circuit and turn on the bulb. Put some goodies in the box and challenge your friends to open the box without switching off the light or damaging the box.

A

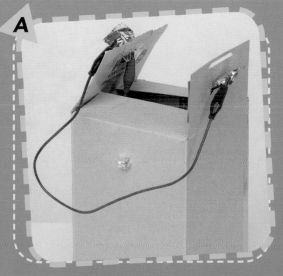

▶ **Observe**
What do your friends do to try and open the box? They will need some wire to complete the challenge (see step A) so have some ready for them. How long does it take them to figure out how to do it?

▶ **What's wrong?**
Foil strips not staying connected? Try pushing them together more firmly, or bending them into shape.

▶ **Record**
Use a camcorder or cellphone to make a movie of your friends trying to open the box.

▶ **Think about it**
How could you make it much harder for your security system to be beaten? How could you add a buzzer to warn you, too?

Magnetic Fields

When real scientists first investigated electricity, they had no idea of its links to magnetism. The discovery was made by accident when a wire carrying electricity was left close to a compass. Scientist Hans Christian Oersted noticed that the compass needle changed position.

When a current of electricity passes through a wire, it generates a magnetic force, like that of a magnet, which spreads out in a region around it. This region is called the magnetic field.

▲ This illustration shows Hans Christian Oersted (1777–1851) from Denmark, standing with an assistant as he made his discovery in 1820.

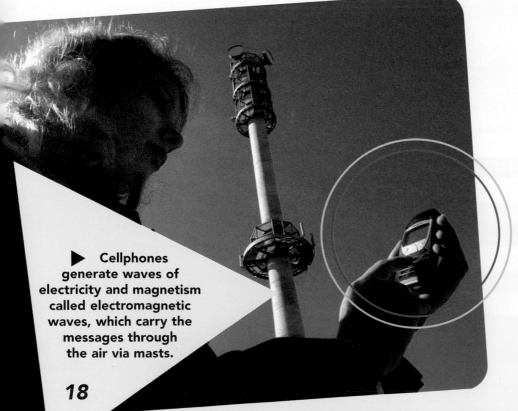

► Cellphones generate waves of electricity and magnetism called electromagnetic waves, which carry the messages through the air via masts.

Get Going

In this investigation you will repeat Oersted's discovery and compare the magnetic field of a magnet with that of an electric current flowing through a wire.

Testing Magnetic Fields

1 Place the mapping compass on a table and let it settle to point north. Move the scale until the N is under the arrow. Bring a fridge magnet near the compass.

Science Box

A fridge magnet, a mapping compass, two batteries, a bulb, a switch, a piece of insulated wire about 40 in. (100 cm) long (strip off ¼ in. (1 cm) of insulated coating at both ends of the wire), two wires with crocodile clips, some batteries from a flashlight or other gadget.

2 Set up the circuit and place one wire over the compass needle. Switch on the circuit.

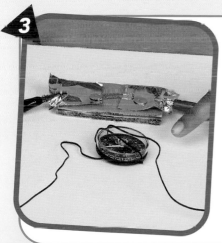

3 Wrap the wire around the compass twice and switch on the circuit. Make sure the north pole of the compass turns to the right. If it doesn't, change the wires around on the battery. Measure the movement of the needle against the compass scale.

▶ **Observe**
What happens when the fridge magnet is brought to the compass needle? What happens when you let electricity flow through a wire over the compass?

▶ **Predict**
Predict what will happen if the wire is wrapped around four times and then five times. Test your prediction. What will happen if you use two batteries? Test your prediction.

▶ **Record**
Write down the number of degrees the north pole points to when there is one, two, three, four, and five coils wrapped around the compass.

▶ **Fair test**
Test 1.5 V batteries from flashlights and see if you can detect a battery that is about to run out of power.

▶ **What's wrong?**
Bulb doesn't light? Check all connections to make sure they are secure. Difficulty reading the needle movement? Make sure the compass points north, then it should be easier to see the deflection.

▶ **Think about it**
The spinning Earth behaves like a magnet. Could you use a compass if the Earth stopped spinning?

4 Repeat step 3 with the wire wrapped three times.

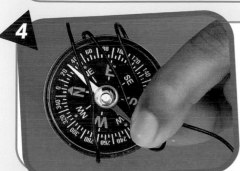

Super Electromagnets

The magnetic field generated by an electric current can be used to change an ordinary piece of iron or steel into a temporary super magnet, called an electromagnet. The magnetic field affects tiny groups of atoms (called domains).

▼Rows of electromagnets are used in Maglev railroads. The electromagnets in the tracks repel against the ones on the Maglev train and propel it at high speed.

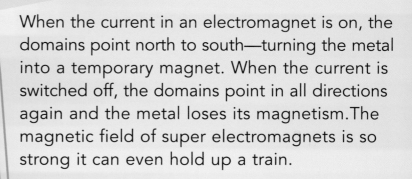

▼ Electromagnets are used in many everyday objects, including car horns and music speakers.

When the current in an electromagnet is on, the domains point north to south—turning the metal into a temporary magnet. When the current is switched off, the domains point in all directions again and the metal loses its magnetism. The magnetic field of super electromagnets is so strong it can even hold up a train.

Get Going

Thumbtacks are made of steel and can be lifted by a magnet. Will a bolt wrapped in a coil of wire carrying an electric current attract the thumbtacks like a magnet? And what happens if you use a bigger coil? Let's find out!

Make an Electromagnet

1
Test the bolt to see that it does not pick up any of the thumbtacks.

Science Box
A steel bolt approximately 1½ in. (4 cm) long, two pieces of thin insulated wire about 16 and 20 in. (40 and 50 cm) long, with ¼ in. (1 cm) of insulation coating stripped off both ends of each wire), two batteries, three wires with crocodile clips, thumbtacks.

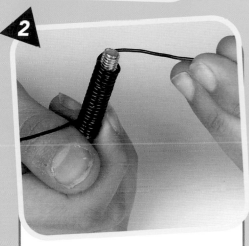

2
Take the shortest wire and coil it tightly around the bolt. Connect the ends of the coil into a circuit with two batteries and let the electricity pass around the circuit. Bring the end of the bolt near to the tacks.

3
Repeat steps 1 and 2 with the 20 in. (50 cm) piece of wire.

4
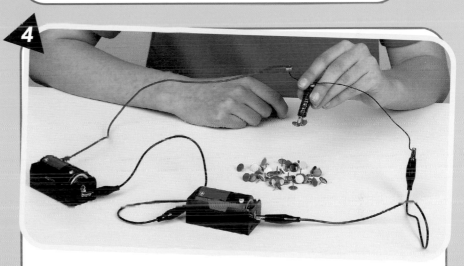

Put both coils on the bolt and join the ends by twisting them together. Now repeat step 2.

▶ **Observe**
What happened when you brought the end of the bolt near the pins when both pieces of wire were coiled around the bolt? Does the coil become warmer or cooler when the electric current flows through it?

▶ **Record**
Photograph the bolt picking up thumbtacks when it has the different coils in place.

▶ **Predict**
What do you think would happen if you increased the number of coils around the nail even further? Test your prediction.

▶ **What's wrong?**
Pins unaffected by the electromagnet? Check all connections to make sure they are secure. Try steel paper clips instead. Make sure the wire coil is neat and tight.

▶ **Extra experiment**
Challenge your friends to see who can pick up the most thumbtacks with their electromagnet.

▶ **Think about it**
How could you move a car in a junkyard?

Generators and Motors

Electromagnets are used to generate electricity at power stations, which supply us with household electricity. Inside each generator is a huge electromagnet, surrounded by a coil of wire. The electromagnet is connected to a shaft that is turned by moving steam or water to generate electricity.

▼ This remote-controlled racing car has a powerful motor that turns the wheels. Some also have motors to power them along.

WARNING!
Household electricity is very powerful and can kill. Never try experiments with it.

A motor has a coil of wire on a shaft surrounded by a magnet. When electricity passes through the wire, it makes the coil behave like a magnet. The magnetic field of the coil "pushes and pulls" on the magnet around it—spinning the coil on the shaft.

Get Going

A motor and a generator are very similar in design, but can you make your own simple motor? Follow the instructions carefully for a spin-tastic result!

1 Wrap the 24 in. (60 cm) wire around into a circle, removing 1 in. (3 cm) of insulation from either end. Rub off the clear coating on the wire with the sandpaper.

Science Box

Five diss (fridge) magnets, two large paper clips, adhesive tape, two 1.5 V batteries and holders, three wires with crocodile clips, sandpaper, marker pen, 24 in. (60 cm) solid-core insulated wire, scissors, a plastic cup.

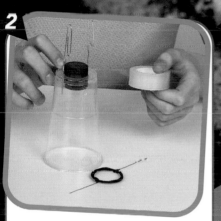

2 Put three of the magnets in the cup and then hold them in place with two on the bottom. Unfold the paper clips and tape onto the cup as shown.

3 Rest the coil in the paper clip cradles. Make sure it spins freely—just above the magnets. Color the top half of one end of the uncoated wire.

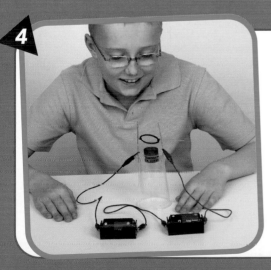

4 Use the sandpaper to rub a patch on each paper clip. Attach the crocodile clip wires to these patches on the paperclips and connect the batteries.

► **Observe**
What happened when you connected the wires and batteries to the motor? Did it start to spin immediately, or did it rock from side to side?

► **Record**
Record the movement of the coil using a camcorder or cellphone.

► **What's wrong?**
Nothing happens when the circuit is completed? Check the connections. You may need to use sandpaper to rub the cradle of the paper clip where the motor axle rests. Still not working? Make sure the axle is straight and that the coil sits just above the magnets, but doesn't touch them.

► **Think about it**
Current flows through the coil, creating an electromagnet. One side becomes a north pole, the other a south pole. The fridge magnets (permanent magnets) attract their opposite pole on the coil and repel their like pole. This attraction/repulsion causes the coil to spin. Why do you need to coat the top half of one end of the wire with the marker pen?

Scientific Circuits

With so many wires, bulbs, and batteries in complicated circuits, it's surprising there aren't more crazy scientists around! But one genius came up with the idea to use symbols instead of drawing all the components in a circuit—especially when things get complicated.

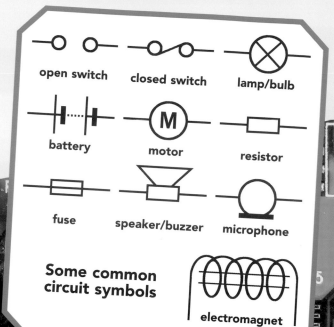

▼ These are the symbols for the components for making simple circuits. The long vertical line on the battery is for the positive terminal on the cap and the short thick line is for the negative terminal on the base.

open switch · closed switch · lamp/bulb

battery · motor · resistor

fuse · speaker/buzzer · microphone

Some common circuit symbols

electromagnet

▲ This circuit board has hundreds of different connections and components.

AD1843JS
BDB5434A-0.3
9732

There are many more small components used in complicated circuits. A cellphone, for example, has a microphone into which you speak and a loudspeaker to let you hear the caller. The games and camera on a cellphone have many tiny circuits with lots of different components to make them work.

Get Going
Can you invent something that needs circuits? Start by making a robot head.

A Robot Head

1 Unscrew the top of the bottle and push on the lump of modeling clay. Push on the motor, keeping the contacts free of clay.

Science Box

A 2 quart (2 liter) plastic bottle, lump of modeling clay ¾ in. (2 cm) in. diameter, a motor, two batteries, switches 2 and 3 (from page 15), six wires with crocodile clips (you may also need some normal wire), a plastic bowl or tray, scissors, adhesive tape, two bulbs, a buzzer, a cereal box, aluminum foil.

2 Push a small hole in the center of the plastic bowl or tray and push onto the motor.

3 Connect the motor to a battery and switch 2. Make sure the bowl, which will be the top of your robot head, can spin freely when the switch is closed. Continues on the next page...

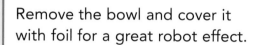

Remove the bowl and cover it with foil for a great robot effect.

Now add a buzzer to your motor circuit as shown—you may need to lengthen the wire so it is not too short. Make sure you connect the red buzzer wire to the positive terminal on the battery.

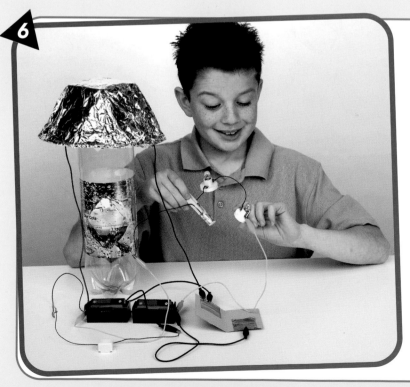

Now things get more complicated! Add the bulbs using a separate circuit. Use switch 3 so that when the circuit is complete the bulbs are on. When you press the peg to break the circuit, the bulbs will go off.

7

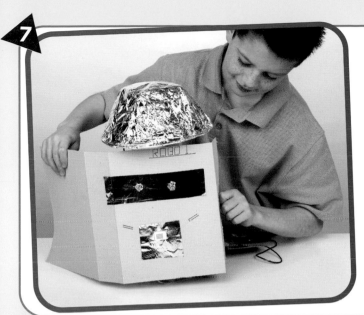

Cut out two eye holes, and a hole for the buzzer from the cereal box. Decorate the front of the cereal box with your robot face. Line up the bulbs and buzzer and stick the cereal box around the bottle. Hide the circuit behind the cardboard.

8

Your robot head is fully operational! Use switch 2 to control the top of the spinning head and the buzzer. Switch 3 controls the eyes—you can make the eyes flash on and off by releasing and pressing the peg.

▶**Observe**

When did the bulbs light and the buzzer sound? Did the bulbs light up more or less when the buzzer and motor circuit was on?

▶**Extra experiment**

This model may give you ideas to make something else. Try out your ideas.

▶**What's wrong?**

Buzzer doesn't work? Make sure the positive contact (red wire) is connected to the cap of the battery. Also check that the connection with switch 2 is on the right side (see step 5). Head keeps falling over? Add some weight to the bottle using sand or stones, or stick the base down with modeling clay. Top of head caught on cereal box and won't spin? Trim the top.

▶**Think about it**

Draw the circuits for the robot face using the symbols on page 24. How could you improve it?

Page 7 Electrical Fleas

Only the glitter fleas and perhaps a few paper ones will jump up at first and stick to the underside of the lid. After you have rubbed the lid again, all the fleas may have jumped up under it and perhaps fallen back, then jumped up again in a kind of dance. If the distance is lower, more of the fleas will jump up at first, some of the others may not dance as much as there is less space for them to move. Something charged with static electricity may have tiny objects sticking to it.

Page 9 A Charge Detector

If the material brought near the foil is charged, it will send an electrostatic force through the air to the foil. This will make the end of the foil nearest the material have the opposite charge to it and be attracted to it. Materials such as stone, wood, pottery, and brick do not become charged when rubbed. The adhesive tape becomes charged by the action of being pulled off the roll. The balloons would have the same charge and move away from each other.

Page 11 A Simple Circuit

The bulb lights when all the connections of aluminum foil are secure. All metals, such as steel, copper, brass, silver, gold, and aluminum, conduct electricity. The graphite in the lead of a pencil also conducts electricity. Rubber, plastic, wood, stone, pottery, and cloth are insulators and do not conduct electricity. If you leave the circuit connected, the battery will run out of power and the bulb will stop shining. Energy is lost by the electrons as they make the bulb shine and this leads to the loss of power.

Page 13 Making Circuits

The motor will spin in step 1, but will not spin in step 2 because the batteries are not facing the same way. In step 3, the two motors spin slightly slower than the single motor in step 1 because they offer greater resistance, or opposition, to the flow of electricity (the push of the batteries). In the extra experiment, you create a parallel circuit. (In steps 1–3 you create a series circuit.) Parallel circuits enable the same power to flow to all parts of the circuit—so the two motors spin at the same speed as the motor in step 1. If you add another battery, you will increase the voltage of the circuit, which will cause the motor to spin faster. Batteries are available in different voltages so the right battery can be chosen for the right component, for example, one or two 1.5 V batteries for a 3 V bulb. Batteries that are not correctly aligned will not power the appliance and could damage its circuits.

Page 15 Make Three Switches

The bulb should light when the paper clip touches both thumbtacks. The bulb will not light until the two pieces of foil are in contact inside the poster board. The bulb will light immediately and only go off when the clothespin is opened. Switch 3 will probably be the best at sending Morse code messages. String could not be used because it is an insulator.

Page 17 Make a Security System

To complete the challenge, the circuit must be extended so that the box flaps can be opened without the bulb going off. This can be done with a piece of wire or foil. To add the buzzer, you need another circuit with another foil switch, a battery, and buzzer. Stick one half of the foil switch to a piece of cardboard under one flap, and the other foil strip to a piece of cardboard on the other side. Arrange them so that when the lid is opened, the foil pieces touch and close the switch, which sets off the buzzer alarm.

Page 19 Testing Magnetic Fields

The compass needle moves. It may be attracted to or repelled by the fridge magnet. Turning the fridge magnet over produces an opposite action. The north pole of the compass needle should move a little to the right when electricity flows in the wire above it. As the number of coils increases, the needle is deflected more and more. When two batteries are used, the compass needle is deflected more strongly. Batteries losing power will deflect the needle less than stronger batteries. If the Earth did not spin, it would not behave as if it had a magnet inside it and the compass would not work.

Page 21 Make an Electromagnet

The bolt at first will not pick up any thumbtacks because it is not magnetized. With the first coil, the electromagnet may not be powerful enough to lift the thumbtacks, but it will be as the coil gets larger. The thin wire heats up as electric current passes along it because of its high resistance. In a junkyard you could move a car by using a huge electromagnet.

Page 23 Make a Motor

If the north pole of the fridge magnet were nearest the coil, for example, it would attract the south pole of the coil when the electricity is switched on. As the south pole swings down to face the fridge magnet, the coating of ink on the wire acts like a switch and breaks the circuit. The part of the coil facing the fridge magnet is now not as strongly attracted to it and because of its inertia (the tendency for everything to keep doing what it is doing—in this case, spinning past the fridge magnet) moves the coil away from the fridge magnet. As it does so, the coating of ink no longer separates the metal of the coil and paper clip and the circuit is switched back on. This makes the next part of the coil a south pole, which is pulled down toward the fridge magnet. This switching on and off makes the coil spin.

Page 27 A Robot Head

The bulbs lit when the switch in their circuit was closed (on). The buzzer sounded when the switch in its circuit with the motor was closed (on). The bulbs could be lit up when the motor and buzzer circuit was on or when it was off. When making extra experiments, do not use more than two batteries in a row when making other models because the bulbs will blow. You could connect the motor directly into the speaker circuit. The circuit diagram for the robot head is shown on the right.

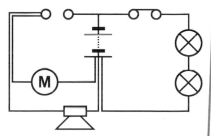

Further Information

Look at these web sites for more information on electricity and how it works things:

▶ *http://ippex.pppl.gov/interactive/electricity/magnet2.html*
This web site looks at static electricity, current electricity, and magnetism—with plenty of animations.

▶ *http://www.kids-science-experiments.com/bendingwater.html*
The simple experiment on this web site uses the power of static electricity to bend water!

▶ *http://www.kids-science-experiments.com/chargedornotcharged.html*
This simple experiment investigates static charge using two balloons.

▶ *http://wow.osu.edu/experiments/electricity/electroscope.html*
This web site from the Ohio State University shows you how to make an electroscope—an instrument used to measure the strength of an electric charge.

▶ *http://www.andythelwell.com/blobz*
Use this crazy "Blobz" web site to check your knowledge of electricity with animations, quizzes, and activities. It might give you ideas for more burglar alarms or other models like the robot head.

▶ *http://wow.osu.edu/experiments/electricity/connectcirc.html*
Keep a steady hand to stop the bulb in this circuit from coming on in this game.

INTERNATIONAL MORSE CODE ALPHABET (see page 15)

A .-	N -.	0 -----
B -...	O ---	1 .----
C -.-.	P .--.	2 ..---
D -..	Q --.-	3 ...--
E .	R .-.	4 ....-
F ..-.	S ...	5 .....
G --.	T -	6 -....
H	U ..-	7 --...
I ..	V ...-	8 ---..
J .---	W .--	9 ----.
K -.-	X -..-	Period .-.-.-
L .-..	Y -.--	Comma --..--
M --	Z --..	

Every effort has been made by the Publishers to ensure that these web sites contain no inappropriate or offensive material. However, because of the nature of the Internet, it is impossible to guarantee that the contents of these sites will not be altered. We strongly advise that Internet access is supervised by a responsible adult.

Glossary

Atoms
Very tiny particles that make up all materials.

Ceramic
A substance containing clay that has been heated strongly and become a hard, brittle material that does not conduct electricity.

Circuit
A loop made by connecting electrical components, such as bulbs and batteries, with wires so that a current of electricity can pass through them.

Conductor
A material that lets an electrical current pass through it.

Contacts
Pieces of metal in a switch that must touch to let a current of electricity pass through a circuit.

Current (electric)
The flow of electricity in a circuit.

Domains
Groups of atoms in iron or steel that can behave like microscopic magnets.

Electrons
Tiny negatively charged particles that form the outer part of atoms and can move through conductors and form a current of electricity.

Insulator
A material that does not allow an electrical current to pass through it.

Magnetic field
The area around a magnet where the magnetic force acts on magnetic materials.

Neutral
A condition in a substance where the positive and negative electrical charges balance and cancel each other out.

Nucleus
The center of atoms where positively charged particles, called protons, are found.

Particles
Very small pieces of a substance (matter). They may be microscopic, or even smaller, such as protons and electrons.

Protons
Positively charged particles that are found in the nucleus of an atom.

Resistance (electric)
A material's opposition to the flow of an electric current, measured in Ohms.

Robust
Sturdy. Does not wear out quickly.

Static electricity
Electricity that stays in one place and does not move in a current.

Terminal (battery)
The place on a battery where a wire is connected to form a circuit.

Versorium
A device for detecting static electricity on a substance.

Index

To my granddaughter Pippa May

This edition first published in 2011 by
Sea-to-Sea Publications
Distributed by Black Rabbit Books
P.O. Box 3263, Mankato, Minnesota 56002

Text copyright © Peter Riley 2008, 2011
Design and concept © Sea-to-Sea
Publications 2011

Printed in China, Dongguan

All rights reserved.

Library of Congress Cataloging-in-Publication Data

Riley, Peter D.
 Electricity / Peter Riley.
  p. cm. -- (The real scientist investigates)
 Includes index.
  ISBN 978-1-59771-279-8 (lib. bdg.)
 1. Electricity--Juvenile literature. I. Title.
 QC527.2.R543 2011
 537--dc22
                                2010005370

9 8 7 6 5 4 3 2

Published by arrangement with the Watts
Publishing Group Ltd., London.

Editor: Susie Brooks
Series Editor: Adrian Cole
Art Director: Jonathan Hair
Design: Matthew Lilly
Picture Research: Diana Morris
Photography: Andy Crawford (unless
otherwise credited)

Acknowledgments:
Mike Agliolo/SPL: 2c, 6. Ulrich
Baumgarten/Vario images/
Alamy: 18b. Vince Bevan/ Alamy: 16r.
Alexander Caminada/Alamy: 1, 3cr, 22.
Darinsh M/Shutterstock: front cover ccr, 3b,
24. demarcomedia/Shutterstock: 2cl. Kevin
Foy/Alamy: 20t. Laurence
Gough/Shutterstock: 2t, 5t. Chris Harvey
/Shutterstock: 4br. Jamuldin/Shutterstock:
3cl, 20b. Patrick Jendres/Alaska
Photographics: 12-13.Jhaz
Photography/Shutterstock: front cover br,
4bl. Ken Kaminsky/Corbis: 4tr.Andre
Klassen/Shutterstock: 8-9.Kerbert
Kratky/Shutterstock: 2br, 14b. Danny
Lehmann/Corbis: 7b. Plasticon Europe BV:
7t. Rolf Richardson/Alamy: 3tl, 16l. Ronen
/Shutterstock: 14t. SPL: 18t. Stephen
Sweet/Shutterstock: 13t.
Every attempt has been made to clear copyright.
Should there be any inadvertent omission please
apply to the publisher for rectification.

March 2010
RD/6000006414/002